MAKE MONEY NOW!™

MONEY-MAKING OPPORTUNITIES FOR TEENS WHO LIKE TO WRITE

MARCIA AMIDON LÜSTED

ROSEN
PUBLISHING®

New York

Published in 2014 by The Rosen Publishing Group, Inc.
29 East 21st Street, New York, NY 10010

Copyright © 2014 by The Rosen Publishing Group, Inc.

First Edition

Library of Congress Cataloging-in-Publication Data

Lüsted, Marcia Amidon.
Money-making opportunities for teens who like to write/Marcia Amidon
Lüsted.—First edition.
    pages cm.—(Make money now!)
Includes bibliographical references and index.
ISBN 978-1-4488-9386-7 (library binding)
1. Authorship—Vocational guidance—Juvenile literature. I. Title.
PN153.L87 2014
808.02'023—dc23

2012044920

Manufactured in the United States of America

CPSIA Compliance Information: Batch #S13YA: For further information, contact Rosen Publishing, New York, New York,
at 1-800-237-9932.

CONTENTS

INTRODUCTION 4

Chapter 1 **SHARING YOUR SKILLS** 7

Chapter 2 **IN THE NEWS** 17

Chapter 3 **IT'S AN INTERNET CONTENT WORLD** 29

Chapter 4 **WORDS ON THE PAGE** 40

Chapter 5 **IT'S A BUSINESS** 50

Chapter 6 **NOW AND LATER** 61

GLOSSARY 66

FOR MORE INFORMATION 69

FOR FURTHER READING 73

BIBLIOGRAPHY 75

INDEX 77

INTRODUCTION

When Christopher Paolini was only fifteen, he thought of a great idea for a fantasy novel. It was about a young farm boy named Eragon, who finds an unusual stone in the mountains. The stone is actually an egg, and a baby dragon eventually hatches from it. This sets into motion events that lead to a quest and a battle between good and evil.

Christopher, who was homeschooled, attempted to write the novel, but he got stuck after just a few pages. He spent the next two years learning everything that he could about the writing process. Then he returned to writing his novel. When he finished it in 2002, his parents decided to help him self-publish the book, titled *Eragon*. The family spent the next year promoting the book. They organized book signings and other events to get people to buy *Eragon*. They even attended Renaissance festivals, where they knew they would find people who liked to read fantasy. Christopher wore a costume and stood behind a table, talking about his book for eight hours at a time.

What happened next was pure luck. The popular author Carl Hiaasen was traveling through Montana and bought *Eragon* at a local bookstore. He gave it to his twelve-year-old son, who enjoyed it so much that Hiaasen recommended the book to his publisher, Random House, one of the largest publishers in the United States. In 2003, Random House published *Eragon*, and it became a best seller when Christopher was only seventeen.

Christopher Paolini's experience with writing and publishing may seem like it was caused by luck. But he was successful mostly because of hard work and the willingness to learn how to be a good writer. As a result, with three more books in the

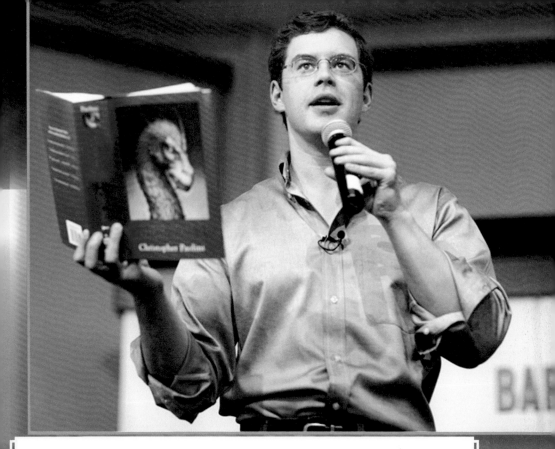

Christopher Paolini reads from his fourth novel, *Inheritance*. His hard work and willingness to learn about writing helped him succeed in the publishing world.

series after *Eragon*, he has made money—lots of money—doing what he likes to do most: writing.

Making money through writing doesn't require selling a book to a big publishing house. There are many ways to make money through writing, and most of them are not nearly as difficult as what Christopher Paolini accomplished. Ethan L., eighteen, has been writing a regular column for *Cobblestone* magazine since he was in fifth grade. He knows how to work with an editor and how a magazine is put together. He makes money writing the column for nine issues yearly. In addition, he has a built an impressive portfolio of published work to use in applying to colleges.

Flip through the pages of your local newspaper or one of your favorite teen magazines. Chances are good that inside its pages you will find an article, a department, an editorial, or even a regular column written by a teen. It might be a book review, an article about a local school event, or a fictional story. In some cases, entire magazines are made up of writing from teen contributors. No matter what the content is, teen writers are actively using their skills and doing something they love in order to make money.

To make money with your writing skills, you don't have to give up all of your free time to market your work. It may not even require getting your work published. All it takes is recognizing that something you are good at—writing—can generate money in many different ways.

CHAPTER
1
SHARING YOUR SKILLS

When trying to find ways to make money, one of the first things to do is to identify your strengths and weaknesses. What do you like to do? What do you do well? If the answer to those questions is writing, then you are already on your way to finding money-making opportunities right now. If you find that writing for school assignments comes to you easily, and you get along well with other students, one of the best ways to start making money with your skills is through peer tutoring.

Peer-to-peer tutoring can be a good way to begin making money using your writing skills.

GETTING STARTED

If tutoring sounds interesting to you, the first step is to check whether your school has a peer-to-peer tutoring system already in place. There are many places where you can tutor other students in writing, but the easiest place to start is in your own school. Tutoring usually takes place on school property, during lunch breaks, free periods, or after school. Some peer tutoring programs operate only for academic credit, and you might participate as part of a class in your schedule. But some schools pay students to tutor other students. Even in a program that does not offer payment, tutoring other students can give you valuable experience. You can use this experience to apply to other, paying tutoring services or to start your own.

When you ask to become a writing tutor, the school will probably take a look at your academic record. It will check to see if your grades are good in English and writing and whether you have received any awards or honors related to writing. You may have to fill out an application and get recommendations from your teachers.

Once you have been accepted into your school's tutoring program, you will be assigned a student or students to work with. The school may have a set of skills for you to teach, or you may assist students with specific class assignments. Typically, a student brings a rough draft of a paper or an essay, and you go through it together to identify what works and what doesn't. The student then revises it and brings it back to the next session. It is important to refrain from rewriting papers for your students. Give them useful feedback instead. Your role is to help students see what would make their writing stronger and what they need to avoid doing. This strengthens not only their academic skills but yours as well.

The process can also have other benefits that you may not have considered. Arif S., who worked as a peer tutor in his

STUDENT PLAGIARISM

With the increasing use of the Internet for plagiarism, the topic is bound to come up in your work with students. The following are some warning signs of plagiarism:

- Someone who hasn't written very well in the past suddenly writes a paper at a much higher level than you've read before, or his or her writing style seems different.

- The formatting of the paper is not consistent. There are sections with different fonts or different margins.

- The paper doesn't quite follow the assignment or address the topic the student was given.

What do you do if you suspect plagiarism? You can check phrases or sentences from the paper (enclosed in quotation marks) in Google or other search engines. If you find plagiarism, talk to the student, or contact the student's parents or teachers to find out what to do next.

school, wrote in *Teen Ink*, "It is a wonderful experience that not only gives a person the satisfaction of teaching another, but it also helps the student more than a teacher sometimes would. Teaching another person something also encourages the peer tutor to be patient, understanding, and sensitive to the student's needs."

You can also tutor students independently outside your school. However, you may find it difficult to get started with new clients if you've never tutored before and lack experience and recommendations. If you are in this situation, you might try tutoring as a community service. This is a good way to build your reputation and gain some personal recommendations from students and their parents.

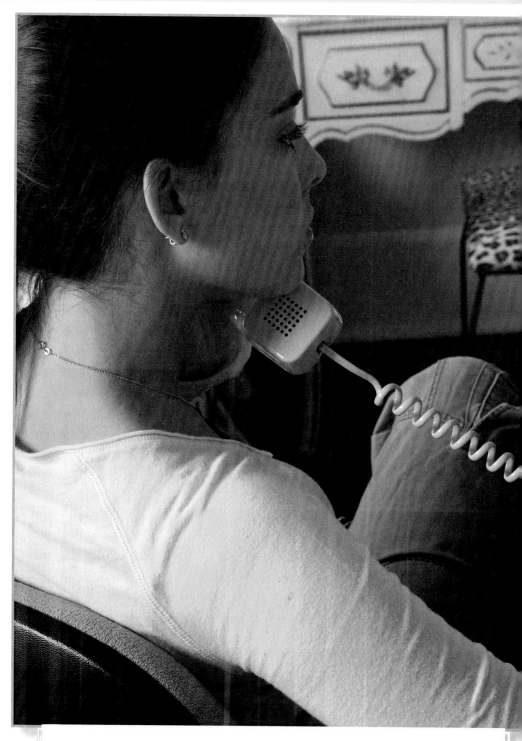

If you're interested in getting a job with a tutoring company, the first step is to call and find out which companies are hiring.

THE NEXT STEP

Perhaps you've been work-ing with your peers through the school's tutoring pro-gram for a semester or a year, either as a class or for community service. Now you'd like to make some actual money for tutoring. There are many companies that employ students to tutor other students. If you have built up your résumé with school tutoring experi-ence, you'll be in good shape to apply to one of these tutoring companies. Your résumé should include your grades and academic hon-ors, as well as your school tutoring experience. Also important are recommenda-tions from your students, teachers, and the admin-istrator who oversees the school's tutoring program. If you have been tutoring privately, include references from your students and their parents. The more proof you have of your effectiveness as a tutor, the more likely you are to be hired by a tutoring company.

Once you have your references and résumé ready to go, the next step is to find tutoring companies that operate in your area and start contacting them. You can start by calling and asking to speak to the manager, and then asking if the company is hiring writing tutors. Be sure to talk about your experience and expertise in writing. Find out if the company hires teen tutors or only adults with college degrees or classroom teaching

Once you have tutoring experience through your school or a tutoring company, you may decide to start your own tutoring business.

experience. If the company does employ teens, you will probably be required to fill out an application for employment and go for an in-person interview. If the company requires your academic transcript for review, you can request this from your school's guidance counselor.

If the manager tells you that the company does not have any openings at the moment, ask if you can send your résumé

to keep on hand for future job openings. It's also a good idea to get the name and contact information of the person who is in charge of hiring so that you can communicate with him or her directly. Be sure to check back with the company on a regular basis, to see if it has any openings and to make sure that your name and information stays visible.

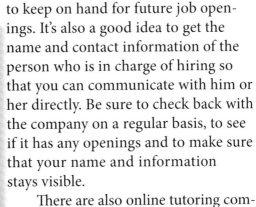

There are also online tutoring companies, and many of them hire teens to tutor other teens. These companies may have more students in need of tutors, since they aren't limited to one geographic location.

ON YOUR OWN

Perhaps you've tutored for your school and then for a local tutoring company, and you feel that you have enough experience to start your own tutoring service. You may even decide to hire other student tutors to work for you, especially if you want to broaden your tutoring to other subjects besides writing and need teens with different academic expertise. You can advertise your service locally, both in schools and in the community. If you charge slightly lower rates than local tutoring companies, you can attract your own clientele.

Erik Kimel started his own private tutoring business in the suburbs of Washington, D.C., when he was a senior in high school, according to an article in the *Washington Post*. His business Peer2Peer Tutors started in 2004 with an ad in the local paper that read, "Students learn best from other students. Any subject. Any grade. Call Erik." His $50 newspaper ad kicked off a company that Kimel continued to run all through college and beyond. By September 2008, he was employing 130 tutors and teaching 176 students, at about half the hourly rate of traditional adult tutors. Today, running the company is Kimel's full-time job, and the company operates in multiple locations across the United States.

WHAT TO WATCH OUT FOR

While tutoring teens or younger students in writing skills can be a good way to make money, there are things to watch out for. Working with peers your own age can be particularly challenging, especially if a student doesn't really want to be tutored but has been forced into it by a teacher or parent. You have to create a working relationship that includes good communication and trust in order to get results.

Successful peer tutoring depends on building a relationship of trust and communication.

It can help to find a shared interest or simply to come to an agreement about the student's goals and how you can best work together. Tutoring may result in a friendship, but this won't always be the case. If you are having difficulty getting your student to cooperate or make any progress, then you need to enlist the help of a parent, a teacher, or an administrator if you're in a school setting, or your supervisor at the tutoring company.

Another pitfall of tutoring is the potential for plagiarism. You don't want to find yourself writing papers or essays for your students, who then put their names on them. Not only is this type of plagiarism wrong, it may also come back to haunt you if the activity ever comes to light. In a school setting, involvement in this kind of cheating can go on your permanent record. It can affect your college applications and perhaps even future employment. It may be tempting to accept payment for writing someone else's paper, but chances are good that you'll pay for it later on with serious damage to your reputation.

Using your writing skills to tutor other students can be a lucrative way to take advantage of something you do well while helping other students who have more trouble. But just as teaching isn't for everyone, tutoring may not be what you want to do. Next, we'll investigate ways to help your writing reach a wider audience.

CHAPTER 2

In the News

O ne of the best ways for teens to make money using their writing skills is in journalism. Journalists research, write, and report news for a variety of media outlets, including newspapers, magazines, television, radio, and the Internet. Most towns and cities have a local newspaper that comes out daily or weekly. There are many pages to fill every time the paper comes out. Editors are continually looking for content that relates to

Because newspapers are published so frequently, they need a constant supply of content. Today, most papers have online editions that can accommodate even more content.

the local area and that will make local readers want to read their publication. Does your school have its own newspaper or journalism club? If you've been working for your school paper, chances are you already have many of the skills you need to write for your local newspaper.

NEWSPAPER WRITING: THE BASICS

Before you start looking for writing opportunities with a local newspaper, it helps to understand some of the basic elements of journalism.

Writing an article or a story for a newspaper involves some very basic questions: Who? What? When? Where? Why? How? These are the questions readers want answered when they read an article in their local paper, no matter what the subject is. Any newspaper story should answer these questions, even if it's just about a school basketball game or theater performance.

In reporting "hard" news, such as stories about crimes or other important events, the article is usually arranged in what is called the inverted pyramid style. This means that the most important part of the story comes first (for example, what disaster occurred), followed in declining order of importance by the other elements of the story (whether people were killed or injured, the extent of property damage, the nature of the emergency response, etc.). These elements should answer the basic questions asked above. It is also important to answer the question "So what?" Explain why readers should be interested in or care about the story.

Above all, a news piece has to capture the reader's interest. So all of this has to be written in a way that's colorful and interesting as well. To enliven a story, journalists usually add "human interest" elements such as interviews, opinions, and eyewitness accounts.

Finally, since journalists are expected to report the truth, the story must be told in a way that is fair and balanced.

LOOKING FOR OPPORTUNITIES

So you're comfortable with the kind of writing that is required for newspapers. Now you'd like to find some opportunities to do this type of writing and get paid for it. The first thing to do is to start reading your local newspaper (or if you live in a larger metropolitan area, newspapers) regularly. Are any reporters regularly covering school news, school sporting events, and other school activities? Does it appear to be the same person who writes all of these stories? Is there a regular department written by a student? Usually a regular department or feature will provide the writer's biography and tell you if the writer is a student or an adult. If you read the newspaper regularly and don't see a student-written column—or any particular attention given to students and school-related topics—then the time is right to propose this coverage.

It will be helpful to examine student-written features in other newspapers, which you can often access online. As you read more of these pieces, you'll get a sense of what students generally write for newspapers and how you can do the same thing for your local paper. Print out some of these columns or clips and use them to show what is possible in a student-written feature.

The person who makes decisions about the newspaper's content is the editor in chief or the editor, depending on the size of the publication. You can usually find his or her name on the newspaper's masthead or on its Web site. This is the person you should contact. Call or e-mail and ask if you can make an appointment to discuss the possibility of writing for the publication. Be sure to mention that you are a student, and be as professional as possible.

You should go into your meeting with the editor with a specific idea of what your department or column would cover. Would it focus on school news? Sports? Extracurricular

Be prepared for your first meeting with an editor by bringing specific ideas and writing samples.

activities? Special events? School-to-community issues? Would it be a weekly department or column or one that only appears in the paper every few weeks? The best way to convince an editor that your idea is valid is to have a serious proposal, written out with specific ideas.

The editor will also want to know what kind of writing experience you have. If you have been a part of your school's newspaper or journalism club, you can show that you have the necessary experience. In fact, if you've participated in school journalism activities, you may have already toured the newspaper's facilities or contributed some writing pieces. Use any kind of writing experience to persuade the editor that you can handle a regular weekly or biweekly writing job. If you have clips (samples of your writing) from a school paper, provide those. If you do not, try writing a sample column or story as if you already had the job. Show the editor how well you write.

Today, most newspapers publish not only a print version of the publication, but an online version as well. Because online content is not limited by the costs of paper and printing, there is

Working on a school newspaper can help prepare you for paid work in journalism.

usually more room for additional information, stories, features, and departments. If your local newspaper cannot spare the room in its print version for a student-written department, ask the editor if he or she would be willing to develop one in the online version.

HANDLING REJECTION

Perhaps you have great ideas and a good writing style, but the editor still turns you down. What can you do now to get your foot in the door of newspaper journalism? You can ask if the paper has any internship opportunities. As an intern, you can work for the paper part-time without pay to gain skills and learn about the publishing process. This can often lead to writing for the paper and perhaps even to a regular job.

Another option is to become a stringer. A stringer is a newspaper correspondent who is not part of a regular newspaper staff but is hired on a part-time basis to report

BE A PROFESSIONAL

If you do find yourself with a regular feature in a newspaper, such as one that involves reporting on school events and issues, you should always present a professional appearance in public. You should dress neatly, avoiding clothing like ripped jeans, flip-flops, or that old T-shirt from your favorite band. Avoid socializing with your friends when you are working on an assignment, and pay attention instead of talking on your cell phone or texting. Listen respectfully to the people you interview. It's a good idea to have a list of questions ready so that you remember everything you wanted to cover. If you are attending a meeting, do some background research on the issues being discussed so that you can ask intelligent questions. You are representing the publication that you are working for, and you want to inspire confidence in people who might provide you with information. If you dress neatly, act professionally, and are attentive at events and meetings, you'll earn the trust of the people you interact with and work for.

It is very important to dress and act professionally when you are representing a newspaper or other publication in public.

on events, often in a particular place. On a very small news-paper, there may not be enough money for someone to write a regular department or column about school-related matters. However, the paper may need someone who can be sent to report on school events or meetings when they occur. This is a great way to gain experience with basic reporting.

THE ANSWER IS YES!

Perhaps the editor loved your idea from the start, or per-haps you've been working for the paper as a stringer or intern and the editor has decided that the time is right for your own feature. What's next? The editor will probably have a very clear set of expectations for what your feature will include, as well as how frequently it will appear and what it will cover. Editors know their readership, and they will want to tailor your feature so that the maximum num-ber of people will read it.

Your editor will give you a word count to follow so that the feature's length fits the paper. You will need to stick to the required number of words as closely as possible, without going too far over or under. There will also be a strict deadline for when your writing must be submitted in order to meet the newspaper's deadlines. The paper may provide a style guide and information about verifying sources, topics to avoid, and other issues. You are responsible for reading and following any guide-lines that you are given.

You may also want to do some job shadowing with another reporter at first. Ask if you can spend a day or several days with a reporter as he or she goes into the community to report on an event or issue. Spend some time watching the reporter do the job. Observe how the reporter approaches people, gathers information, and then writes about it. This kind of on-the-job

To start training for a journalism career, you can shadow an experienced reporter on the job.

training is extremely valuable when you're getting started. An experienced reporter can show you how to sift through the information you've gathered and determine what is accurate and what is gossip or unverifiable information. He or she can also show you how to find accurate information when it's difficult to discover.

Newspaper journalism is a skill that teen writers can use to generate income right now. It can also lead to similar writing at the college level and even in the professional world. It is real-world writing, and if you love to talk to people and be in the thick of the news, it may be the perfect fit for you.

CHAPTER 3

It's an Internet Content World

The Internet is a vast place, with an insatiable hunger for new content. Did you ever wonder where all the content you read online comes from? The owners of Web sites create some of that content. But even more of it is created by freelance writers. This makes writing for the Web one of the best opportunities for teens who want to make money by writing. If you write well, especially if you can write on popular topics, you can make money writing online content. You can build a professional writing portfolio at the same time. The best part is that you can do this from home, whenever you want.

The drawback to writing online content as a teen, however, is that some sites will not pay you for your writing until you are eighteen years old. However, if you're interested in getting your writing out there and visible, as well as building a portfolio of your work, it may still be worthwhile to write for a Web site even if you are not getting paid.

As a general rule, you should always have a parent or guardian check out any Web sites for which you are considering writing content. It's important to be sure you want your name associated with a particular site. In addition, writers are often required to sign up on a site and establish a PayPal account for receiving payment. So it is always best to have an adult check the site for you before you proceed. Some sites also require you

Writing for the Internet is one of the best opportunities for teens to make money using their writing skills.

to be a certain age before you can contribute content or be paid. Read the fine print so that there won't be unpleasant surprises.

THE BIG THREE

There are a huge number of sites on the Web that need content. The best way to start is to find a site that is set up to purchase content from freelance writers. There are three major sites that teen writers have used to make money: Helium, Triond, and Yahoo! Voices (formerly called Associated Content). All three of these sites purchase content from freelance writers, but the way they work is slightly different.

HELIUM

Helium is a content site that asks writers to submit articles on almost any subject. These articles are immediately posted on the Web site. But you don't earn money from your writing right away. You earn money when people read and rate your articles. A good article will get positive reviews and show up in many online search engines.

Payment comes from three factors: how good the article is, how valuable the topic is, and how much Helium's advertisers

IT'S ALL ABOUT REPUTATION

The Internet may be the land of opportunity for writers, but it's also a much smaller world than many people realize. Remember that any time you put your name to something on the Internet, there is a chance that it will come back to haunt you. Be sure to publish only your best work, and never write anything that you might someday be ashamed of. Any piece of writing with your name on it represents you.

will pay to place ads on the topic. Every time someone clicks on your article, you receive a certain amount of money. That money will accumulate for as long as the article remains posted, sometimes for years. However, the amount of money you are paid for clicks on your article is usually very small, and you won't receive payment until you have reached a certain dollar amount, such as $25. Many writers believe that the real benefit of Helium is the feedback you gain from user reviews and the comparison of your writing to other people's writing. This can help you improve your style as well as build an online writing portfolio.

On the Helium Web site, young writer Wesley Kaye commented on his experience writing for the site: "Helium is an awesome place to be for all types of writers. I have just started my writing career and enjoy all Helium has to offer in order to make an extra buck while doing something I truly love. I hope to be a journalist in the future, and Helium will help me build a very nice portfolio of my work. I hope to be here for a very long, long time."

TRIOND

Triond is another online site that solicits content from freelance writers, as well as photographers and composers. The site has a three-step process. First, the writer creates original and unique content. Triond's employees review the content for quality and, once they accept it, publish the content on the most relevant Web site within their network of sites. (These include sites related to poetry, business, sports, health, travel, and wellness.) Then the writer earns revenue.

Unlike jobs that require you to be in an office every day, writing content for the Internet can be done anywhere and at any time.

Making money with a Triond article depends on the number of people that click on and view your article and the ads featured near it. It is also based on a referral system that pays you if you recommend Triond to others. Triond's reviewers will reject articles that they feel aren't up to the site's standards. However, they will give the writer the opportunity to make revisions based on their suggestions and then resubmit the article.

With both Helium and Triond, the writer isn't going to make a great deal of money unless he or she writes a huge number of articles every month. Writers gradually discover which topics are the most popular and tend to generate the highest number of viewings and revenue. An advantage of Triond is that it creates a writer's network in which you can get to know other writers and communicate with them.

YAHOO! VOICES

Another money-making site for freelance writers is Yahoo! Voices, formerly known as Associated Content. Like the other sites, Yahoo! Voices publishes articles on certain topics and pays writers according to the number of page views and advertising clicks. Unlike at Helium and Triond, however, reviewers at Yahoo! Voices evaluate an article right after the writer submits it and make a payment offer based on what they think the article is worth. The writer doesn't have to wait for the article to receive traffic before being paid for it but will earn additional money based on its popularity. Payments can continue for years if an article is popular enough. The site also maintains an "assignment desk," or a list of topics that it is seeking writers for. A writer can claim an assignment and write an article about the topic. This can help writers target subjects that are most likely to generate page views and revenue. In time, a writer who produces strong work can be named a

THE BIG NO-NO

Unfortunately, there is a large market on the Internet for people who will write papers for students to purchase and pass off as their own. It might be tempting to join a Web site that promises to pay you to write term papers and do other academic writing for students. However, not only is this unethical, coming under the category of academic dishonesty, but many colleges and universities are actively trying to shut down these "essay mills." If your name is linked with one of these organizations, it could have serious consequences in the future when you try to get a job. And do you really want the burden of knowing that you're helping someone else cheat and that your writing might be used for illegal or unethical purposes?

"preferred content producer" and may be offered assignments that pay more than the regular rate.

MORE OPPORTUNITIES

If the idea of writing articles isn't appealing, there are other ways to make money online using your writing skills. Some sites will pay teen writers to write reviews of products. For example, sites such as SharedReviews.com pay writers to review products from beauty supplies to video games.

There are also sites for teen writers who are very good at writing letters. These sites, such as LetterRep.com, allow users to submit letter requests. Freelance writers then create a custom letter based on a request. Users can also access existing letters, everything from letters of resignation to love letters. Writers are paid for each custom letter they write. They receive additional money if the same letter is purchased again in the future.

Many small businesses are in need of writers who can help maintain their presence on Facebook and Twitter.

Writers can make as much as $10 for a custom letter and for each future use of the letter.

Teen writers can also write online content for local businesses. For example, small businesses like stores and restaurants may have their own Web sites but lack the time to continually generate fresh content. Succeeding in this market requires organization and effort on the part of the writer. Constructing a Web site or creating advertising materials may be necessary to generate business. It can also be worthwhile to visit local businesses and ask if they have a need for this kind of service. When approaching business owners, it is helpful to have a business card and writing samples to share.

Some smaller companies may also need writers to post regularly on Facebook or Twitter for them. These postings are most effective when made daily, and they may require more time than the company has. If you are very comfortable with social media sites and can write content related to the company's business, this can be a great job.

Finally, if you love to blog, you can set up your own blog site

Making money by writing online content requires hard work, but if you can commit to writing and posting regularly, it can be a good source of income and help you establish your writing career.

and then place pay-per-click advertisements on it as a way to generate income. However, this is effective only if you blog about something that generates enough interest to lead to many advertising clicks.

IT'S HARD WORK

The key to making money online as a teen writer is simply hard work. With most content sites, you'll need to write a large number of articles in order to generate a reasonable amount of money. But if you can commit to spending time every day writing and then posting your articles, you can not only make some money but also establish yourself as a writer with a visible portfolio. The best part is, you can accomplish this without having to get dressed up or even leave home!

CHAPTER 4

WORDS ON THE PAGE

Maybe you are drawn to more traditional types of writing, where you actually see your words printed on the pages of a magazine or even in a book. Freelance writing—writing stories or articles and then finding places to sell them—is less predictable and more difficult than other types of writing work, but it can pay better and is a great gateway to a future professional writing career.

Freelance writing for magazines follows a certain process. The writer writes a story, article, or poem and then looks for a market where it might be published. Typically, writers can submit their writing in two ways. They can either send in an entire piece of writing, or they can query an editor at a magazine or publishing house. This means they write a letter presenting an idea in the hope that the editor will like the concept and want to publish the work. If a magazine accepts a piece of writing, it is published months later, as magazines generally work as much as a year ahead of a specific issue. Payment may occur when the piece is accepted or not until it is actually published.

As a way to earn money, traditional freelance writing can be very hit or miss, since you must first create a piece and then find a place to sell it. The process is similar in book publishing, which can be even more difficult. Because books are long and expensive to publish, book editors must be very choosy.

HOW MANY ISSUES A YEAR?

For many writers, writing for magazines is a good way to break into the business. A typical magazine must fill its pages with content month after month, or even weekly. This makes the odds of selling your work to a magazine better than selling to a book publisher because magazines need new content all the time.

Magazines also publish a wide variety of content. No matter what subject you're interested in writing about, be it science fiction, gaming, movies, horses, or extreme sports, chances are there's a magazine about it. The content can also take many different forms, from traditional stories and articles to interviews, personal experience pieces, reviews, commentaries, and travelogues. You can choose to write about something you're interested in and then try to sell your piece. Or you can take a look at a magazine's list of themes for upcoming issues (usually found on the magazine's Web site) and try to write something to fit a theme. Be sure to give plenty of lead time, as magazines are put together many months before they are actually published.

Magazines also have regular departments or features, but for a teen writer, getting one can be difficult to achieve. Ethan L., who has written a Web review department for *Cobblestone* magazine since fifth grade, happened to be in the right place at the right time. He was also eager enough to take advantage of an opportunity. Ethan had always been interested in U.S. history (the focus of *Cobblestone*) as well as in how magazine publishing worked. When the magazine's editor gave a presentation to his classroom about *Cobblestone*, Ethan saw an opportunity, approached her, and said that he was interested in writing for the magazine. After talking with him, the editor was impressed and decided to give him a chance. At first, he wrote book reviews, and then he worked on finding online content related to each issue's theme. Out of his interest came eight years

Because magazines are published so frequently, they require a great deal of content on a wide variety of subjects.

of regular writing as well as the opportunity to be a student adviser for the magazine.

GETTING STARTED

If you are interested in developing a freelance writing career with magazines, where do you start? The first thing to do is make a list of magazines that publish writing by teens. You can find many of them online simply by searching for magazines that accept teen writing. You can also use a magazine market guide, available at your local library or bookstore. There are several of these: some are aimed at people who write for children and some are aimed at people who write for adults. Market guides for children's writers usually have a section that specifically discusses markets for young writers.

Whatever guide you decide to use, read through the listings carefully. Note what each magazine publishes and whether it accepts work only from writers of a certain age. Some magazines are paying markets and some are not, so you must decide if you're only willing to write for pay or if it's more important to you to create a body of published work.

WRITING CONTESTS

Don't forget contests! There are many contests that recognize the work of talented teen writers. Categories include fiction, nonfiction, essays, opinion pieces, and more. Some organizations actually hand out cash prizes for winning writing, and others award scholarships. While some contests just offer publication, winning them gets your writing into the public eye and looks impressive on your résumé or in your portfolio. Search online to see what contests are out there and how you can enter.

Entering your work into writing contests can be a great way to win cash and scholarships, as well as an excellent opportunity to get published.

Once you have identified some possible magazine markets for your work, study each magazine and its guidelines for writers. If possible, find hard copies of a magazine at a local library or bookstore, and examine them to see what kind of articles and stories it publishes. Also note the overall tone of the magazine. Are its articles light and funny? Are they written in a casual, or even trendy, style? Or is the magazine serious and formal in presentation and tone? Only by actually reading a magazine can you get a feel for it and decide whether your writing would fit. It is possible to read parts of some magazines online, but these samples may not give you the complete "flavor" of the magazine. (Of course, if you're thinking of an online-only magazine or e-zine as a market, you should read the entire issue electronically.)

Every magazine has a set of guidelines for potential writers. Magazines specify what kinds of writing they publish and what the general word counts are for their content. It is important to pay attention to these points. If a magazine publishes only stories of eight hundred words and you send in a three-thousand-word story, the chances of the story being accepted are pretty slim.

The guidelines also explain how to submit your work to the magazine. Some editors require you to query your idea first. This is especially true for magazines that have a specific theme for each month's issue. Other editors just ask you to send the entire story or article, sometimes by e-mail and sometimes by regular postal mail. Be sure to follow these guidelines exactly because an editor who asks only for e-mail submissions may overlook a postal mail submission. No matter how you send your submission, be sure that it looks as professional as possible.

Once you have submitted a story or article to a magazine, you must be prepared to be patient. Responses can take a long time, and these days, some magazines won't respond at all if they decide that your writing isn't a good fit for them. Resist the urge to call, e-mail, or write to ask about your submission, as

For many young writers, the ultimate dream is to publish a book of their own. It's rare for teens to sell books to large publishers, but it is a wonderful goal for the future.

it is unprofessional and can be annoying to an overburdened editor. If you want to make sure that your submission got to the magazine, it's acceptable to include a self-addressed, stamped postcard that the editor can easily drop into the mail, letting you know that your work was received.

A WORD ABOUT BOOKS

Writing a book and having it published is the ultimate dream of many teen writers. And it might seem like the best way to make a great deal of money quickly. But in reality, there are several reasons why teens don't routinely have books published by traditional book publishers. The number-one reason is that a teen's writing simply hasn't matured enough to be published. Even the most promising young writers can look back at their work years later and be critical of their early efforts. Book publishing is also an extremely competitive field, particularly in a poor economy. Publishers want books that are guaranteed to have a large audience, and it is difficult to sell books by unknown teen writers. Many book publishers won't even consider work by teen authors for these reasons.

TO MARKET, TO MARKET

There are some excellent magazine markets for young writers, and they can be great places to get your first publishing credits. Even though many of the markets do not pay young writers for their submissions, they can start you on the path to becoming a professional author. Be sure to check out each magazine's Web site and read some sample stories and poems. Make sure that what you plan to submit matches the magazine's style and content. Some good magazine markets for teen writers include:

- *Cicada* (http://www.cicadamag.com). This magazine showcases stories and poems written for and often by young adults. Its Web site has a section called The Slam, where teen readers can submit their writing.

- *Claremont Review* (http://www.theclaremontreview.ca). This literary magazine publishes high-quality stories, poems, and plays by writers ages thirteen to nineteen.

- *New Moon Girls* (http://www.newmoon.com). Most of this magazine's content is written by girls, and a team of girls edits the content.

- *Polyphony H.S.* (http://www.polyphonyhs.com). A national student-run literary magazine for high school writers and editors, this publication showcases student fiction, nonfiction, and poetry.

- *Skipping Stones* (http://www.skippingstones.org). A nonprofit magazine for writers ages eight to sixteen, *Skipping Stones* celebrates different cultures.

- *Stone Soup* (http://www.stonesoup.com). This magazine contains writing and art by young people ages eight to thirteen.

- *Teen Ink* (http://teenink.com). *Teen Ink* includes a literary magazine, Web site, and books, all written by teen writers.

Self-publishing is increasingly popular, and it may seem like an easy way to turn your work into a book. However, it can be difficult to actually make any money with a self-published book. Because these books have a reputation for uneven quality, many bookstores are reluctant to carry them. And unless you are prepared to spend a great deal of time promoting and marketing your book, it is unlikely that you will sell very many copies. Most self-published books only ever sell a few hundred copies at most, even though they may be available on sites like Amazon and Barnes & Noble. And as self-publishing proliferates, it will likely become even more difficult to get your book noticed.

Many writers believe that shorter pieces of writing, such as those intended for magazines, are a good way to hone writing skills and build a body of published work. These samples can come in handy later when submitting query letters to book publishers. Freelance writing for print may be tougher than online content writing, and often more frustrating, but the satisfaction of seeing your words on a physical page is hard to beat.

CHAPTER
5

IT'S A BUSINESS

No matter what kind of writing you do, for newspapers, magazines, Web sites, or other online content, you must remember that writing professionally is a business like any other. There are certain things that you must attend to in order to conduct yourself professionally and make a good impression on your clients.

SPELLING *DOES* MATTER…AND OTHER THINGS, TOO

There are some basic rules to follow in formatting and submitting professional writing. Maybe you're used to doing your writing longhand, with pencil or pen on paper. This might be fine for brainstorming a first draft, but you should never submit anything handwritten to an editor or publisher. Submitting work via e-mail, which is increasingly common, makes it almost impossible to send handwritten stories or articles. However, some companies still accept manuscripts via regular mail. Avoid the temptation to send in notebook pages of a scrawled, handwritten twenty-page story.

There are also certain formatting rules that you need to follow when typing your work. Always double-space your lines and use a ten- or twelve-point font. Resist the urge to use a fancy font. Instead, stick to something simple like Times New Roman, Courier, or Arial. Readability is the key. Editors read for a living, and a piece of writing in an ornate font—or in a color other than black—is harder on their eyes. Also, print only

Spelling and grammar are extremely important in professional writing. Don't rely on your word processing program to locate errors.

on one side of the paper to make your writing easier to read and edit. Don't forget to include your contact information on the first page. Number your pages, too, in case they get mixed up.

If you're used to writing on a computer, you may not give much thought to spelling and grammar, assuming that the computer's spell-check and grammar-check programs will catch any mistakes. However, you can't rely on these tools. Spell-check doesn't always catch words that are spelled correctly but used incorrectly. Sometimes it auto-corrects words, changing them into something very different than you intended. You must be very sure to proofread your writing before submitting it. Not only should you proofread it right after you finish writing, but you should also let the piece "cool" for a day or two and then reread it. You'll be amazed at what you might have missed the first time.

EDITOR ETIQUETTE

Another important aspect of becoming a professional writer has to do with etiquette. You need to use your best manners in your dealings with editors, publishers, clients, peers, and anyone else you come into contact with as a writer. Remember, you are starting a business, and it's vital to act in a professional, businesslike way. Always pay careful attention to deadlines: If an editor or client tells you that a piece of writing has to be done by a certain date, then treat that as an unbreakable deadline. Don't tell yourself that you have plenty of time and then end up scrambling at the last moment. That is a stressful situation, and it can result in poorly written content. One of the fastest ways to lose writing jobs is to miss deadlines. This is especially true with magazines and newspapers, which often have hard-and-fast schedules for content delivery and production. Always meet your deadlines, and if

Carefully tracking schedules and always meeting deadlines are among the most important habits of a professional writer.

you can do so with a few days to spare, that will only help to build your reputation with clients and result in more business in the future.

Remember to act like a professional in your interactions with editors and clients, too. Respect the ways that people want to be contacted, and communicate clearly and appropriately. If you're submitting to a magazine as a freelance writer, you should not call or e-mail incessantly to check the status of your submission. As long as you have included all of your contact information, editors will get in touch with you if they are interested in publishing your work. And remember the truth in submitting as a freelance writer: No news generally means "No, thank-you." If you don't hear back about a submission after a few months, it most likely means the editor is not interested in the piece.

WHAT AM I WORTH?

Some of the publications you might write for, such as online content sites or magazines, will have set payment rates. They may calculate their rates per word written, or for the writ-

STYLE GUIDES

For some writing jobs, you may be asked to follow a certain style guide. This usually means a professional, published style guide such as the *Chicago Manual of Style*, the *Associated Press Stylebook*, or the *MLA Handbook*. A style guide sets out the "rules" of things like capitalization, punctuation, grammar, and citing sources. Most of these guidebooks can be found at your school or local library, or they can be purchased (although some are fairly expensive). They are also accessible online, usually for a fee. The plus side? When you go to college, you may have to follow a certain style for your academic writing, so you may be ahead of the game.

ing project as a whole. But some clients may ask what your rate is per hour of writing. The best way to handle this is to find out what other writers are charging for similar work and then set your rate accordingly. Remember, as a teen it's a good idea to set your rates lower than those of more seasoned professional writers, to attract the business you need to build up your career.

It is also important to keep track of the time you spend writing. Most writing is done for a set rate, regardless of the time spent, but some companies expect you to charge according to the number of hours you worked on a writing project. As you track your progress on different projects, which we'll discuss in the next section, you should record the exact number of hours you spend on each. Even if you aren't being paid an hourly rate, it will help you establish just how long different kinds of projects take you to complete. This will help you get a sense of how much you are earning for your time and will help you plan for future projects.

KEEPING TRACK

An important aspect of being a professional writer is keeping track of your work. You need to create a tracking system for all of your submissions and assigned work. That way you'll know, for example, if you submitted a piece to a publication so long ago that you can assume it was rejected. Then you can send it somewhere else.

Spreadsheets work well for keeping track of what you have sent out, when you sent it, and to whom you sent it. They also work well for keeping track of assigned work. Create a chart that lists the writing you have been assigned, when it is due, and where it should be sent. By checking these spreadsheets daily, you'll always have a clear picture of what is due and what you have finished.

You should also keep track of payments and not rely on various publications or businesses to make sure that you are paid. For every piece of writing that you sell, list the date of the invoice (bill) and the payment amount due to you. Then check it off when it has been paid. You may want to create an invoice template on your computer for clients that don't have their own invoices. You can adjust the template for the job you are doing. This will ensure that your payment isn't forgotten, particularly if you are working for local businesses creating Web content. Even with larger companies, sometimes payments fall through the cracks. For this reason, it's important to know exactly what is owed to you and whether it has been paid.

At first, you may not earn enough in a year of writing to need to file taxes, but if you do, your payment spreadsheet will also be a clear record of what you earned and from whom. Any time you receive payment, you should keep the check stub or a printout of the payment history from a source such as PayPal, as a record of your earnings. A file folder is the best way to collect these financial documents for the year.

CONTRACTS

Eventually, most writers will have to sign a contract for a specific piece of writing. A contract is a formal agreement between the writer and the organization buying the writing. It spells out exactly what is expected of both of you. The contract usually addresses the question of rights to the work. When you sell a piece of writing, you are selling someone the rights to use that writing, but the nature of these rights can vary.

Most magazine contracts work in one of two ways. The magazine may buy all rights to the work. This means that the publisher owns the piece and can do whatever it wants with it, even reprint it over and over again. Or, the magazine

It is important to read and understand a writing contract before signing it. Pay particular attention to what rights you are selling.

may have first rights, which means it has the right to publish the piece the first time, but you may be able to resell it after that.

Other types of publications vary as to what the publisher is buying and how long it can use your writing, so you need to be certain that you read the contract very carefully before signing it. It should state exactly what the company is purchasing from you. Remember, if you sell all rights, then you cannot resell that same piece to someone else. Doing so is illegal and can get you into serious trouble. If you are not sure what a contract is saying, ask your editor to explain it or get help from an adult, preferably someone who has experience with legal language. There are also online sources that can help you decipher the sometimes confusing language of contracts.

It might be tempting to ask for more money or different rights when you're given a contract to sign. Obviously, if you feel the terms are unfair, you should try to work out something else. But be aware that when you are just starting out in your writing career, it can be more important to get your writing in print for your portfolio than it is to argue over payment and rights. You run the risk of having the editor say, "Never mind."

GET YOURSELF OUT THERE

Finally, remember that as a writer starting a business, you need to advertise your services. This can be as simple as using your computer to create business cards and a brochure of the services you offer. These can be handed out to prospective clients, such as local businesses that might need your writing skills, or even posted on a bulletin board. If you have enough experience, you can create a résumé that lists what you have written and what companies you have worked for. Your word processing program most likely has templates for creating a résumé, as well as other materials such as business cards and advertisements. You can also get the help of a local printing company if you want to spend more money.

It's important that you present yourself professionally in your advertising. Stay away from cutesy images, distracting fonts, or phrases like "aspiring author." Include your name, address, e-mail, phone number, and Web site if you have one. Plain and simple is best.

You should also create a portfolio of your published work. This can be a file folder or a loose-leaf binder with plastic page

Marketing tools such as brochures and business cards can help you present yourself professionally and advertise your services.

protectors. The portfolio allows a prospective client to browse through your work. Some book and magazine editors require "clips" with a submission or query. A clip is simply a copy of anything that you've written and published professionally. You can access these from your portfolio when you need to. You should also keep some of your clips in digital format so that they can be attached to an e-mail submission easily. (If necessary, you can digitize print documents with the help of a scanner.)

Becoming a professional writer is an exciting process, but it does take work. You want to do everything you can to advertise yourself and create a solid reputation. After all, this is your business!

CHAPTER
6
NOW AND LATER

If you've worked hard and had some luck, when high school comes to an end, you will have the start of a nice career in writing. You may be tutoring peers in writing, developing online articles, or writing a monthly feature in your local newspaper. Now you're thinking about college. What's next?

USE THOSE SKILLS

You've got terrific writing skills, and you've accumulated published clips and know how to work with editors or clients. All of these things can help you write a great college application essay and hopefully win you acceptance at the school of your choice. If you hope to major in creative writing or journalism, you can use some of your published clips as part of your application.

Many college courses are heavily dependent on writing, so your honed writing skills will help you move through your college years more easily. Being a fluid and skillful writer will help with your overall academic success.

You can also continue to use your skills as a way to make money while you're in college. Most colleges have writing centers where students can go for help with papers and essays. With strong writing skills and experience, you have a good chance of being hired to work there and tutor other college students. If you've found success with freelance writing and online content development, those are also easy to continue while you're in college. You can adjust your freelance writing workload based on how much time your academic work takes and how much time you are willing to allot for your paid writing.

You may decide to pursue your writing career by taking journalism, English, or creative writing classes in college. To make money, you may be able to tutor in the school's writing center.

If journalism is the type of writing you enjoy most, you can join your college's newspaper or yearbook, or even contribute to its Web sites.

No matter what path you decide to take in college and beyond, your experience making money with writing, and the

INTERNSHIPS IN PUBLISHING

As a high school student and especially as a college student, one way to gain experience in writing and publishing is through an internship. Many publishing companies offer internships to students. They may not be paid positions, but for several months during the school year or summer break you can help put together a magazine or see how books are created. You may even get the chance to have your writing published in a magazine or on a Web site, under your byline, which is a great way to start building a portfolio. Most publishers' Web sites tell you if they accept interns and explain how to apply for these positions.

Internships with magazines and publishing companies can give you valuable experience and perhaps the chance to see your writing in print.

way you've polished your writing skills, will serve you well. Almost every type of business needs people who are good at communicating in writing. For example, if you decide to pursue marketing as a career, your skills can help you with commercial copywriting. Strengthening your writing skills early on helps set the stage for future success.

VOLUNTEERING

Remember that applying your writing skills can be about more than just making money. Perhaps you'd like to share your writing skills with people who need them, simply as a community service or as a way to contribute to a cause that you believe in. Many nonprofit organizations need good writers to help them. Volunteering gives you the opportunity to share your skills for a good cause and also add to your résumé of published work. Are you interested in organizations that work for human rights, environmental advocacy, animal protection, or other issues? Is there a homeless shelter or food pantry near you? These kinds of organizations may need someone to write a newsletter for them, but they may not be able to afford to pay a writer to do it. They may need someone to update their Facebook page on a regular basis or create e-mail news reports. These are all excellent opportunities for using your writing skills and benefitting the community at the same time.

Do you belong to a church, synagogue, mosque, or other religious group? Are you a member of a youth group? Perhaps you can use your writing skills to start a members' newsletter. Or you might contribute to an existing newsletter with articles about young people and their activities. If you are part of a local dance troupe, theater group, or musical performance group, it might need someone to write press releases or promotional materials. And don't forget that you can use your writing and tutoring skills to work with underprivileged children for free. There are many ways to use your writing skills as a volunteer, and you'll make a solid contribution as well as continue to build your own skills and portfolio.

What it comes down to is this: if you love to write, you can use your skills and your enthusiasm for the craft of writing to earn income and contribute to your community. And people who can make money doing what they love to do are the luckiest people of all.

GLOSSARY

CLIENT A person or group that receives the professional services of an individual or business.

CONTRACT A written agreement between two or more parties that is legally binding.

DEPARTMENT A recurring section in a magazine.

EDITORIAL A piece in a newspaper or periodical that presents the opinion of the publisher or editor.

ETIQUETTE Conventional rules for proper social behavior.

E-ZINE An electronic (Internet) magazine.

FEATURE A newspaper or magazine article devoted to in-depth coverage of a special topic, usually not tied to breaking news.

FONT A set of letters, numbers, and symbols that share one design; typeface.

FORMATTING The general appearance of a piece of writing, including font style and size, line spacing, and margins.

FREELANCE To sell work or services by the hour or by the project, instead of working as a regular employee for a single employer.

INSATIABLE Not capable of being satisfied.

JOURNALISM The occupation of collecting, writing, and editing news for presentation in the media.

LUCRATIVE Profitable or money-making.

MASTHEAD A statement printed in every issue of a newspaper or magazine, giving publication information and the names of owners and staff.

PLAGIARISM The act of presenting someone else's words or ideas as one's own.

PORTFOLIO A collection of a person's best creative work, organized to display his or her skills, especially to a prospective employer.

PRESS RELEASE A statement or announcement of a newsworthy item that is distributed to the press, often to generate publicity.

PROLIFERATE To grow or increase rapidly.

PROMOTION The act of publicizing or advertising a product, institution, or cause.

PROOFREAD To read and mark corrections in a piece of writing.

PROPOSAL The formal suggestion or presentation of a plan, scheme, or idea.

QUERY An inquiry, usually in the form of a letter, from a writer to an editor proposing a story, article, or book idea.

RÉSUMÉ A written outline and description of a person's educational and professional qualifications and experience.

REVENUE The income produced by a given source.

SELF-PUBLISHED Published and distributed independently by the author.

SOLICIT To seek something, as in a job or a business transaction.

SUBMISSION A piece of writing that is submitted to an editor or publisher for possible publication.

TRAVELOGUE A piece of writing describing a travel experience or trip.

UNETHICAL Morally wrong, or against accepted standards of professional or social behavior.

VERIFY To prove that something is true or correct.

FOR MORE INFORMATION

Alliance for Young Artists & Writers
557 Broadway
New York, NY 10012
Web site: http://www.artandwriting.org
This nonprofit organization identifies teens with exceptional artistic
and literary talent. It presents the Scholastic Art & Writing
Awards, in which teens have the chance to earn scholarships
and have their work exhibited or published.

American Society of Magazine Editors (ASME)
810 Seventh Avenue, 24th Floor
New York, NY 10019
(212) 872-3700
Web site: http://www.magazine.org/asme
The American Society of Magazine Editors is the principal organization for magazine journalists in the United States. It offers a
magazine internship program for college students, as well as
programs and events to support entry-level journalists.

Associated Press (AP)
450 West 33rd Street
New York, NY 10001
(212) 621-1500
Web site: http://www.ap.org
The Associated Press is a leading newsgathering organization that
offers internships in various forms of journalism, including
print, video, and photojournalism.

Canadian Authors Association (CAA)
74 Mississaga Street East
Orillia, ON L3V 1V5

Canada
(866) 216-6222
Web site: http://www.canauthors.org
The Canadian Authors Association is dedicated to promoting a
flourishing community of writers across Canada. The organization offers conferences, workshops, and other resources for
Canadian writers.

Columbia Scholastic Press Association (CSPA)

Columbia University
Mail Code 5711
New York, NY 10027-6902
(212) 854-9400
Founded in 1925, CSPA unites student editors and faculty advisers
working with them to produce student newspapers, magazines, yearbooks, and online media. The association offers
educational conferences, idea exchanges, critiques, and award
programs.

826CHI

1331 N. Milwaukee Avenue
Chicago, IL 60622
(773) 772-8108
Web site: http://www.826chi.org
This nonprofit organization is dedicated to supporting students
ages six to eighteen with creative writing and expository
writing skills.

International Writing Centers Association (IWCA)

c/o Nathalie Singh-Corcoran, President
English Department

West Virginia University
Morgantown, WV 26505
(304) 293-9731
Web site: http://writingcenters.org
The IWCA fosters the development of writing center tutors, direc-
tors, and staff by sponsoring meetings, publications, and other
professional activities; by encouraging scholarship connected
to writing center-related fields; and by providing a forum for
writing center concerns.

National Scholastic Press Association (NSPA)

2221 University Avenue SE, Suite 121
Minneapolis, MN 55414
(612) 625-8335
Web site: http://www.studentpress.org/nspa
A nonprofit educational association, the NSPA provides journalism
education services to students, teachers, media advisers, and
others. It provides information on developments in journalism and student media and provides a forum for members to
communicate with others and share their work.

Poetry Institute of Canada

P.O. Box 44169
RPO Gorge
Victoria, BC V9A 7K1
Canada
(250) 519-0446
Web site: http://www.youngwritersofcanada.ca
The young writers' division of the Poetry Institute of Canada offers
contests and opportunities for publication to young Canadian
writers ages seven to eighteen.

WriteGirl
1330 Factory Place, Unit F104
Los Angeles, CA 90013
(213) 253-2655
Web site: http://www.writegirl.org
WriteGirl is a nonprofit organization that offers high school girls
mentoring and workshops on the craft of creative writing. It
pairs professional women writers with girls for weekly mentoring and monthly workshops and publishes an anthology of
members' best work each year.

WEB SITES

Due to the changing nature of Internet links, Rosen Publishing has
developed an online list of Web sites related to the subject of this
book. This site is updated regularly. Please use this link to access
the list:

http://www.rosenlinks.com/MMN/Write

FOR FURTHER READING

Barr, Chris. *The Yahoo! Style Guide: The Ultimate Sourcebook for Writing, Editing, and Creating Content for the Digital World.* New York, NY: Yahoo!/St. Martin's Griffin, 2010.

Berger, Sandra. *Ultimate Guide to Summer Opportunities for Teens: 200 Programs That Prepare You for College Success.* Waco, TX: Prufrock Press, 2007.

Brewer, Robert Lee, ed. *2013 Writer's Market.* 92nd annual ed. Cincinnati, OH: Writer's Digest Books, 2012.

Christian, Darrell, Sally A. Jacobsen, and David Minthorn. *Associated Press 2012 Stylebook and Briefing on Media Law.* 47th ed. New York, NY: Associated Press, 2012.

Day-MacLeod, Deidre. *Career Building Through Blogging* (Digital Career Building). New York, NY: Rosen Publishing, 2008.

Dunn, Jessica, and Danielle Dunn. *A Teen's Guide to Getting Published: Publishing for Profit, Recognition, and Academic Success.* 2nd ed. Waco, TX: Prufrock Press, 2006.

Evans, Julie A. *Journalism* (Craft of Writing). Tarrytown, NY: Marshall Cavendish Benchmark, 2012.

Facts On File. *Writing* (Discovering Careers). New York, NY: Infobase Publishing, 2012.

Flath, Camden. *Freelance and Technical Writers: Words for Sale* (New Careers for the 21st Century: Finding Your Role in the Global Renewal). Broomall, PA: Mason Crest Publishers, 2011.

Gibaldi, Joseph. *MLA Handbook for Writers of Research Papers.* 7th ed. New York, NY: Modern Language Association, 2009.

Hambleton, Vicki, and Cathleen Greenwood. *So You Want to Be a Writer? How to Write, Get Published, and Maybe Even Make It Big!* New York, NY: Aladdin: Beyond Words, 2012.

Harper, Elizabeth, and Timothy Harper. *Your Name in Print: A Teen's Guide to Publishing for Fun, Profit, and Academic Success.* New York, NY: St. Martin's Griffin, 2005.

J. G. Ferguson Publishing Company. *Journalism* (Careers in Focus). 2nd ed. New York, NY: Ferguson, 2011.

Lewis, Beth A. *How to Start a Home-Based Tutoring Business.* Guilford, CT: Globe Pequot Press, 2010.

Mazer, Anne, Ellen Potter, and Matt Phelan. *Spilling Ink: A Young Writer's Handbook.* New York, NY: RB Flash Point/Roaring Brook Press, 2010.

Schwartz, Tina P. *Writing and Publishing: The Ultimate Teen Guide.* New York, NY: Scarecrow Press, 2009.

University of Chicago Press. *The Chicago Manual of Style.* 16th ed. Chicago, IL: The University of Chicago Press, 2010.

Zinsser, William. *On Writing Well: The Classic Guide to Writing Nonfiction.* 30th anniversary ed. New York, NY: HarperCollins, 2009.

BIBLIOGRAPHY

Bailey, Jonathan. "3 Reasons to Suspect a Student of Plagiarism." Plagiarism Today, June 28, 2011. Retrieved July 22, 2012 (http://www.plagiarismtoday.com/2011/06/28/reasons-suspect-student-of-plagiarism).

Camenson, Blythe. *Careers in Writing* (McGraw-Hill Professional). 2nd ed. New York, NY: McGraw-Hill, 2008.

Chorlian, Meg. Interview with the author. August 2, 2012.

Delta State University. "Plagiarism Detection & Prevention: A Guide for Faculty." Retrieved July 22, 2012 (http://www.deltastate.edu/pages/1270.asp).

De Vise, Daniel. "Teens Tutor Teens at Student-Created Firm." *Washington Post*, September 7, 2008. Retrieved July 23, 2012 (http://www.washingtonpost.com/wp-dyn/content/article/2008/09/06/AR2008090602881.html).

Helium, Inc. "Writer Testimonials." 2012. Retrieved August 4, 2012 (http://www.helium.com/content/helium-community/writer-testimonials).

Internet Based Kids. "Teens—Writing for Profit." July 22, 2009. Retrieved August 4, 2012 (http://internetbasedkids.com/2009/07/teens-writing-for-profit).

King, Stephen. *On Writing: A Memoir of the Craft*. 10th anniversary ed. New York, NY: Scribner, 2010.

Lemire, Timothy. *I'm an English Major—Now What? How English Majors Can Find Happiness, Success, and a Real Job*. Cincinnati, OH: Writer's Digest Books, 2006.

Peterson, Matthew. "Christopher Paolini—Online Radio Interview with the Author." TheAuthorHour.com, January 21, 2010.

Retrieved July 21, 2012 (http://theauthorhour.com /christopher-paolini).

Sambuchino, Chuck, ed. *Children's Writers & Illustrators Market 2013*. 25th annual ed. New York, NY: Writer's Digest Books, 2012.

Smith, Hilary. "Self-Publishing Success Stories: Christopher Paolini." StyleMatters Writing Services, December 2, 2011. Retrieved July 15, 2012 (http://style-matters.com/blog /self-publishing-success-stories-christopher-paolini.html).

Teen Ink. "Peer Tutoring—Teen Community Service Essay." Retrieved July 22, 2012 (http://www.teenink.com/hot_topics /community_service/article/4065/Peer-Tutoring).

Thomson Reuters. "Reporting and Writing Basics—Handbook of Journalism." 2012. Retrieved July 25, 2012 (http://handbook .reuters.com/index.php/Reporting_and_Writing_Basics).

Waryncia, Lou. Interview with the author. July 22, 2012.

Wiehardt, Ginny. "Publications for Young Writers—Young Writers Publish Their Creative Writing." About.com. Retrieved August 4, 2012 (http://fictionwriting.about.com/od /thebusinessofwriting/tp/Teen-Publications.htm).

Yager, Fred, and Jan Yager. *Career Opportunities in the Publishing Industry*. 2nd ed. New York, NY: Checkmark Books, 2010.

INDEX

A

academic transcripts, 13
advertising, 14, 31, 34, 37, 39,
    58, 60
Amazon, 49
assignment desks, 34
Associated Content, 31, 34
Associated Press Stylebook, 54
auto-correct, 52

B

Barnes & Noble, 49
blogs, 37, 39
book publishers, 4, 5, 40, 47
book signings, 4
bookstores, 4, 43, 45, 49
book writing, 4–5, 40, 41, 47, 49
business cards, 37, 58

C

Chicago Manual of Style, 54
Cicada, 48
Claremont Review, 48
clients, dealing with, 9, 14, 50, 52,
    54, 55, 56, 58, 60, 61
clips, 19, 21, 60, 61
Cobblestone, 5, 41
community service, 9, 11, 64
contests, 44

contracts, 56–58
copywriting, 64

D

deadlines, 26, 52, 54

E

editor etiquette, 52, 54
Eragon, 4, 5
essay mills, 35
e-zines, 45

F

Facebook, 37, 64
fonts, 9, 50, 58
freelance writing, 29, 31, 32, 34, 35,
    40–47, 49, 54, 61

G

Google, 9
grammar-check, 52

H

Helium, 31–32, 34
Hiaasen, Carl, 4
hourly rates, 54–55

I

internships, 23, 26, 63
interviews, 13, 18, 25, 41
inverted pyramid style, 18
invoices, 56

J

job shadowing, 26, 28
journalism clubs, 18, 21

K

Kaye, Wesley, 32
Kimel, Erik, 14

L

L., Ethan, 5, 41
LetterRep.com, 35
letter writing, 35, 37, 40, 49
libraries, 43, 45, 54
literary magazines, 48

M

magazine writing, 5, 6, 17, 40–43,
    45, 47, 48, 49, 50, 52, 54, 56, 60,
    63
market guides, 43
mastheads, 19
MLA Handbook, 54

N

New Moon Girls, 48
newsletters, 64
newspaper writing, basics of, 18

O

online content, writing,
    21, 23, 29–39, 41, 45,
    49, 50, 61

P

Paolini, Christopher, 4–5
PayPal, 29, 56
Peer2Peer Tutors, 14
plagiarism, 9, 16
Polyphony H.S., 48
portfolios, 5, 29, 32, 39, 44, 58,
    60, 65
press releases, 64
proofreading, 52
proposals, 21

Q

query letters, 49

R

Random House, 4
rejection, handling, 23, 26

reputation, managing your, 9, 16, 31, 54, 60
résumés, 11, 12, 13, 44, 58, 64

S

S., Arif, 8–9
scholarships, 44
self-publishing, 4, 49
SharedReviews.com, 35
Skipping Stones, 48
social media, 37
spell-check, 52
Stone Soup, 48
stringers, 23, 26
style guides, 26, 54

T

taxes, filing, 56
Teen Ink, 9, 48
tracking systems, 55–56
travelogues, 41
Triond, 31, 32, 34

tutoring, 7, 8–9, 11–16, 61, 65
Twitter, 37

V

volunteering, 64–65

W

word counts, 26, 45
writer guidelines, 45
writing, making money through,
    business basics, 50–60
    journalism jobs, 17–28, 62
    overview, 4–6
    skill sharing, 7–16
    while in college, 61–65
writing centers, 61
writing samples, 21, 37, 48, 49

Y

Yahoo! Voices, 31, 34–35

ABOUT THE AUTHOR

Marcia Amidon Lüsted is the author of over 70 books and 350 magazine articles for young people, as well as an assistant editor for Cobblestone Publishing's six magazines. She has a bachelor's degree in English, with minors in secondary education and music, and has taught eighth-grade English and worked as a bookseller and book reviewer. She has been writing since she was a child. She knows firsthand that a writing career can take many different forms, from writing books and articles to educational materials, online content, and marketing copy. She is also an instructor for the Institute of Children's Literature, teaching courses in both magazine and book writing. She helps beginning writers hone their craft and find ways to make money doing what they love to do—just as she does.

PHOTO CREDITS